Telepathic Communication

With the Animal Kingdom

D1227946

Telepathic Communication
With the Animal Kingdom

Catherine L. Ceci

ParkerHouseBooks.com

Book design: Candi Parker

Editor: Judee Light

Published by ParkerHouseBooks.com

For

Hears Like Wolf

What People Are Saying...

"So many of us have Animals with which we wish we could talk. Cathy made that happen. She communicated with our Sheena and showed us ways to make her happy and healthy again." -- Dr. Julie Schindler

"Cathy has great intuitive insight concerning horses' needs and what is needed to make them content. As a dressage rider, competitor and Instructor, I find this information very valuable to horse and rider." -- Patti O'Sullivan - Certified Riding Instructor, Florida

"Cathy is one of the most intuitive, gentle and insightful healers I've worked with. Her loving heart brings healing and insight to those she works with. I encourage you to gain the benefit of working with Cathy!" -- Kelly Powers, Intuitive Counselor (Kellypowers.com)

"Cathy is able to offer Horse lovers practical and intuitive insight into their relationship with their horses. You will enjoy working with her." -- Dan Kirkland, Horse Trainer

Acknowledgements

With heartfelt thanks to

Dr. Richard and Liz Powers, Patti Cota-Robles of eraofpeace.org, Horse Trainers Dave Jones and Daniel Kirkland, Rev. Jerry Frederick and Rev. Maeda Jones of Cassadaga, Rev. Ben Cox, Pastor of The Chapel of Spiritual Light in Orlando, Fl, Kelly Powers, Ruby T. Ong, Candi Parker and every person who has loved and grieved the loss of a friend, and took the time to tell me their story.

Foreword

There are special people who hold a larger place in their heart for animals. To them animals aren't "just animals," they are "animal people" as many Native Americans refer to them. They recognize animals as a part of the sentient beings on the planet bringing mankind a gift. Catherine Ceci is one of those people.

She has written this book for others like her who love their animals as deeply as they love their family. Those who know the special relationship that exists between them and their animal friends will resonate as she shares the story of her special gift of communication with animals, how it unfolded, what it offered her life and the others to whom she provided her skills.

In this book, she shares true stories of intuitive messages she has received from both the living and, extraordinarily, the dead, from both human and animals in her life. Her unique qualifications as a respiratory therapist in emergency rooms where death became very much a part of her daily life called her to study the bigger questions about life and death. From the stories she heard from patients, to personal experiences, she explored and came to understand the energetic body that is contained within all living species and she provides a special expertise in this incredible, petite book. Catherine traces, in a very broad sense, the significance our animal friends offer to humans.

I am by profession a licensed mental health counselor and during 12 years of my 25-year career, I worked in bereavement as a grief counselor for hospice. From that perspective, I can say Catherine beautifully described the intricate journey of grief following loss. And as I write books of a spiritual nature, I can verify the stories Catherine shares about both human and animal communication post life.

I, too, had an intimate relationship to many special horses. I am trained as an equine assisted growth and learning facilitator and utilized horses as partners in therapeutic relationships with people for counseling. Many of my human family died during the last 10 years and I've also grieved the loss of horse friends as well.

She once did a reading for a horse I was caretaker of and quite correctly discovered he had a toothache without ever touching him. She introduced me to her friend in China where she was sought after as an animal communicator and I could follow her career through many of her client's stories. Catherine may open an unopened package for many when she gives instructions for developing an intuitive relationship with animals.

There are unique issues that come with the death of a beloved animal and Catherine, as one of those gifted animal lovers, provides a roadmap for the grieving pet owner and for those around them who might not understand. She normalizes a process that is often overlooked and misunderstood by those who are not as connected to the animal world. She even shares ways in which a beloved animal may bring signs for their owner assuring them of their continued state of energetic existence in the same way human beings can send signs. Catherine provides a model to reach beyond the veil and communicate with beloved animals and people, a model of opening intuition that is easily understood. She also provides 'how to' advice if you too want to begin a practice as an animal communicator or just improve your own communication with your pet.

~ L. Shannon Anderson

Author of Parallel Universes: A Love Story Transcending Death and The Magdalene Awakening: Symbols and Synchronicity Heralding the Re-emergence of the Divine Feminine

Contents

Introduction

Watching my horses from a window in my home, it has become clear to me just how diverse people's beliefs are. Mention telepathy to some people and they want to run from you. Mention it to others, and they fully embrace the concept and even practice it. This book is for everyone. Its purpose is not to convince you of the concept of telepathy or change your religious beliefs; its purpose is to share with you my own personal experiences. Everything we witness and experience is a perspective based on one's own beliefs. Some people have difficulty understanding the concepts of telepathy because they live a strictly mental existence. If they can't see it and touch it, then it does not exist to them. My approach is "in my father's house are many mansions..." I invite you to journey with me, through the mansions I have visited.

Although we share many commonalities as humans on this planet, our gifts are found in our uniqueness. Just as we each have a unique set of fingerprints, we also have a unique soul. We can add our gifts and knowledge to this sacred web of life or we can choose not to. It is up to us. This book is my offering. And it is with great humility that I share.

All of the stories are true. Names, of course, have been changed to protect privacy.

My Journey as an Equine Communicator

My journey as an Animal Communicator began in 1996. One day, as I sat on the deck outside of the house where I was living in Lady Lake, Florida, I wrote down on a piece of paper that I wanted to work as an Animal Communicator, especially with horses. I held it up to the sun and said, "Look, God, this is what I want to do to help animals." That night, in a state of half-awake and half-asleep, I saw in my mind's eye a large whale coming toward me. His eyes were looking right at me, and then he shot a red light into my forehead! It was profound. I had never had an experience like that and was not particularly connected to dolphins and whales. It was horses that I felt a strong kinship with.

The next day, at the Cassadaga bookstore while walking around and visiting, I saw this book called *Dolphin Tribe* by Ashleea Nielson and it had pictures of dolphins on the cover. I picked it up and opened to a page where the author described how she had the exact same experience as I did with a whale! Quickly, I looked at the publishing date of her book, and it was two years before. So, I bought the book and it is here next to me as I write. I have yet to let the author know how much her book and sharing of this extraordinary experience means to me, but I plan to. It is the only book I have ever read on Telepathic/Interspecies Communication—although there are many others now.

After reading her book, I had business cards printed up and started with rodeos and other local horse shows offering my services for free. After a short time, people started offering to pay me and, I remember with a smile, that it was the cowboys who first asked me to communicate with their horses at a rodeo. Back then, I often got just one-word answers from the horses such as: curious, lazy, happy or unhappy, interested, not engaged, sore, tired, willing and unwilling. The cowboys would pull money out of their wallet and thank me for "talking to their horse" for them—for helping to solve an issue they were having and, if nothing else, entertaining them! It really was fun and I told myself then to keep it fun always. They found the information their horses were revealing most interesting and they coined me a horse psychic. We had a lot of good laughs over the answers from the horses. I had to tell one cowboy his horse did not like him at all! He laughed and said, "You are right about that...well, tell him I am about to give him to my nephew anyway!"

Next were the barrel racers. By then, more information was coming to me, so the consults expanded as far as what I received. I actually met a horse who said his story was that he did not like women. When I first heard this I thought this cannot be true! But when I told the owner, he said it was right on. Good thing this horse's owner was a guy! This was really getting fun for me and I was living a dream, helping horses and people. I was very excited about Telepathic Communication with the Animal Kingdom and loved sharing what I was learning.

Preparing a "how-to sheet" I would give it to my clients should they ask for more information, I became excited about helping others discover this part of themselves and help the animals in this way.

Equine Communication—Try it

Arrange a meeting with a horse (or dog or any animal you want to try with) that you have never met or heard anything about.

If it is a horse, have the owner halter the horse and be sure to stand in a safe spot near the horse.

Close your eyes and pay attention to what is coming into your thoughts.

What are you feeling from the horse, what images do you see?

Start with a personality reading of the horse. This is reflected in their eyes.

Is this horse funny? Is he/she happy? Grouchy? Just honing into the eyes of a horse can reveal a lot of information.

Are you feeling any pains in your own body, perhaps

indicating the horse is in pain? Where?

You can ask the owner if they have noticed any discomfort in an area on the horse's body, but do not diagnosis a medical condition.

Are you receiving any mental pictures from the horse's past? Can you translate into words to the owner what you are seeing or feeling?

After about 3-4 minutes of this communication, tell the owner everything you felt. This conversation is usually enlightening for the horse owner and you may be surprised yourself that you are spot on.

Word spread and the next few years took me across America and a sponsorship to China. I never turned down any inquiries from the media and there were many media interviews with major networks along with an offer from a major TV show. It never crossed my naïve mind that they were just curious! I gave workshops and seminars to humane societies and regularly taught both mainstream students and the metaphysically minded. From 1996 to about 2002, I was either giving workshops or travelling, but mostly in my truck going from barn to barn giving private consults for people and their horses. I could hardly keep up with the appointments. Back then, most of them were made via phone or e-mail. There were no social utilities, private messages or GPS devices and I got lost a lot. People heard about what I was doing and there were two articles in our local newspaper on my work as well as an interview from a TV station in South Florida, which really opened the floodgates of consults.

Driving to a barn for horse consults was usually a relaxing experience for me. One particular day I felt stress and could not identify the source. I kept dropping things as I drove—directions to the barn just jumped out of my lap, my water bottle seemed to have turned into a Mexican jumping bean and kept falling out of my hand drenching me, the little bit of coffee I allowed myself, which always stayed in the holder, spilled and fell all over my feet and then my cell phone fell into the crack of the seat. I pulled my truck over to the side of the road and commanded to the universe, "What is going on?!"

I gathered myself by taking some slow, deep breaths to clear my thoughts and energy—energy that seemed to be making everything go awry. After a few minutes, I heard these thoughts in my mind and felt these feelings:

"Gather yourself! This barn you are going to is full of stress and sorrow; the client is unfocused and something sad has happened there." I then felt a sharp pain in my knee and a cold, shivering cold, on this hot Florida summer day. With my air conditioner blasting away, sweat was pouring down my face. I looked up at the beautiful roadside and the lush pastures before me. Then, all of a sudden, the lush green pasture looked sad and lonely, and I felt the stench of death that I am all too familiar with from years of working in an emergency room. "Pain, suffering and sorrow," I thought to myself. I wanted to cancel the appointments. I wanted to turn around and go home.

A subtle thought crept its way into my heart as tears were rolling down my face. "You are stronger than this; you are here to help the horses that come into your life. To do that, you must stay connected to yourself to work with the people; drive on."

So, I did; and I was greeted at the barn by a woman who, even before she introduced herself, hugged me. It was a long hug, and as she held me close to her I could feel her heart beating rapidly as though she had just been rescued from imminent danger. She released her grip on me and then, holding me by my shoulders, looked into my eyes.

When people look me in the eye, it does many things to me. Sometimes I feel afraid (just like a horse), sometimes I feel drained and sometimes I feel love. I braced myself for the emotions I knew would follow such an intense gaze into my private world—just as a horse must feel when a stranger approaches (*Canine World Magazine* said of me: "She has eyes which could speak"). I was preparing myself for whatever message or feeling I might receive from this woman who so kindly greeted me. All of this going on in one hug—I sensed that I was her last hope regarding her horse, which is often the case. People usually call me after they have exhausted other resources.

While I was processing all of these emotions, my mind, just like a CD with many tracks, caught the fact that I had thought of the *Canine World Magazine* editorial about me...and briefly, I pondered why that thought would come to me? Before I could completely formulate the words to speak (speaking is sometimes hard for me because my mind works in images and pictures) I blurted out: "Did one of your animals just recently pass away?" She hugged me again, sobbing this time.

"How did you know?" she asked between her gasp for air and crying.

"Because I feel the hurt," I answered. "And I care. We are all connected to one another and to the animals. I am not psychic; I am just extremely sensitive to energy.

I try to take the time to listen and feel. Like a lot of other people, I have a deep love for animals. It is that love, I believe, that opens one's heart to know what the animals are feeling. Sorrow is a strong emotion and one I easily connect with."

We then made our way to her horse in his stall, where, I bet you can guess, his right leg is injured. The pain I felt in my own knee on the way to the barn; I connected the dots and I could see I was receiving information even before I arrived. Hurt, pain and sorrow, very strong energies, can often be felt from a distance. Many people have experienced that with a loved one. Love is such a powerful energy, perhaps the most powerful energy that exists. The thoughts that were coming to me on the way to the consult were trying to tell me this consult was also about her dog that passed. The key word was canine. Learning the language of energy is always like putting together a puzzle!

The story was that right after her dog that she'd had for fifteen years passed away, she was riding her horse over the jumps, as she frequently did, and something happened. What exactly, she did not know. But in the process, her horse fell to the ground injuring his right leg. When I communicated with the horse, I received images of the bit too tight in his mouth along with him tripping over something. He got off balance and down he went. She said she remembered him tripping. She also checked her bit and saw someone else had used it and it was much tighter than she normally set it.

When I told the lady the information I received, she said, "You know, I was riding him right after my dog passed, my mind was in a million directions and I was grieving. I think you are correct, Catherine. I was out of balance and transferred it to my horse." What a lesson!" she exclaimed. "It is okay," I responded, "we all have lessons to learn, and that includes me! We just have to remember that the horses sense and feel what we are feeling and we should never take our mind off them when interacting with or riding them." Her horse eventually healed and the lady and I became friends.

Sometimes it just takes some time spent with someone who has gone through sorrow—sometimes a hug, understanding and your love can help them heal. Thus were my days on the road giving consultations.

After a few years, I stopped. I was at a crossroads. Life was happening too fast for me and I fell back on my license as a Certified Respiratory Care Therapist. I went back into the workplace with the idea that I needed a break and should start putting some of the stories to paper. The idea was a good one, just punch a clock, work with a consistent paycheck coming in and write my book. But the stress of working in the medical field, especially the emergency room, took its toll on me.

I have worked in intensive care units, emergency rooms, nursing homes and rehabilitation centers and witnessed monumental amounts of pain, suffering and sorrow. I always wondered why humans would add more sorrow to the world when there is so much already. Of course, I realized that the majority of people do not, and never will, witness what I and my coworkers saw on a daily basis. The twenty years I spent working in a city hospital watching the results of car accidents, drownings, sudden deaths, and people experiencing the loss of their loved ones, were years of sadness for me. I spent more and more time alone and with my animals, because I felt helpless about the suffering I saw and I did not know how to go about life. I felt socially awkward and it made it hard to be around most people.

During that time, I lost my best friends to death. Dave Jones, the famous horse trainer, saddle maker, and author of several books on horse training, was my mentor and friend. I lived at his horse training stable for years. I watched, listened and assisted as the horses came through for training.

Unknown to most, Dave was a deeply spiritual man and an artist. His saddles were exquisite as he hand sewed them all. His knowledge regarding horses surpassed that of anyone I had ever heard of, and he always told me when we got a new horse in for training to "just ask the horse" what the problem was. He firmly believed, and often stated, "People will lie, or they don't have the knowledge to know what to tell you about the horse, so just listen to the horse." He did not mean only body language; Dave taught me to quiet my mind by breathing deep and listening while standing with the horse and looking into the horse's eyes.

On one of the many days we spent together in his saddle shop, he told me to sit down and close my eyes and start breathing deeply. I did, and I felt him place his thumb on my forehead. He held it there for several minutes then told me to open my eyes. Dave, the cowboy, horse trainer, saddle maker, this was his way of imprinting me to open up my senses. He was proud of the work I was doing with the horses, and he designed my business cards, too.

After that, my life partner, my Dano, was in a car accident and he too passed away.

By this time, I was experiencing overwhelming grief, and then both of my dogs, Kyla and Nina, passed.

Having been around death most of my life, as I started my career as a Respiratory Therapist (former EMT) in 1975, I had sat at the bedside of countless patients with their families as they watched their loved one pass away. I always felt my own heart hurt as I tried to comfort and support families during this extremely difficult time. I sat at the bedside of both of my parents as they passed away. Feelings of loss, grief, and hurt were pretty much the emotions I lived with every day.

But the passing away of my dogs, well, that was a different and a much harder situation for me. As I sit here typing, I search to find the words that can even come close to a description of how it feels.

Death, a Transition into the Dimensions of Light.

But something happened following the "death" in two of these situations—one with my life partner, Dano, and the other with my dog friend, Nina. *They communicated with me during their transition of dying and following their death.*

To give you a better understanding of these experiences, I think it is helpful for you to know more about me. I was foaled in Jamestown, NY, into a non-horse family. (What was God thinking?) As a young child, I was sent to live with my Great Aunt in the country, but then later taken back by my biological parents to the city. Now, today, on my land in the country, I teach Archery, but most of the time I can be found helping someone with their horse.

When I lived with my Great Aunt I had horses, goats, cows, chickens and pigs and lots of dogs and cats. I had plenty of company. I can remember being four years old and riding my horse. I completely remember the feeling I had, and I knew then that being with a horse was all I wanted to do. Living there in the country on the farm was magical to me. When I was about seven years old, my Aunt would sometimes need things from the little store, which was about three miles away, so I would saddle up my horse and ride those three miles with a burlap bag tied to my saddle to get whatever we needed. Riding my horse to the store that far really instilled in me a passion for being alone with a horse. It also taught me how important it was to have a close relationship with a horse, and the only way to be close was to spend time with them. The level of trust my horse, Dan, and I had was beyond anything I ever got to experience again with human or animal.

Imagine in today's world that you could spend ten to twelve hours a day just with your horse. Riding, eating lunch, watching him/her graze, riding some more, playing in the pasture, swimming through ponds and running errands! Just enjoying life together. Most problems I see today with horses and their owners is that they do not spend enough time together. I wince when I see someone riding their horse and talking or texting on their cell phone. When I was a little girl, we did not have a phone in the house. If I wanted to make a call, I had to ride my horse that three miles to the little town to use the pay phone!

In those days, going to church on Sunday was mandatory. I hated it. I hated it because from the beginning I felt out of place in the Sunday school class. I was just a child, but what they were telling me did not seem right. Things such as "animals do not have souls" and "when you die you go to this place called Heaven but animals are not allowed there." I did recall a Biblical statement the Sunday school teacher expressed. It was this: "In my Father's house are many mansions..." When I asked the Sunday school teacher what that meant, she replied, "I really do not know."

I remember one Sunday when I was a bit older, I faked being sick and got to stay home while the rest of the family went to church. I was told since I did not go to church, I could not be seen riding my horse by the community people for that would reflect on the family as somehow being irresponsible towards their faith.

That day a rebel was born inside of me. A non-conformist, as my Aunt used to call me. After they left for church, I saddled my horse and rode two miles to the church, rang the big church bell outside, waved at the congregation and off we ran at a gallop! I know it embarrassed my Aunt, and that is my only regret. But inside of me was an angry girl. Angry because my heart told me these very people who lacked respect for the animals were not people I wanted to be around. As unhappy with me as I believe my Aunt pretended to be, my punishment was that I could not ride my horse at all the next week. But I saw her laugh when she told the story to a relative, and she did not hold to the punishment.

By the time I was thirteen I was stealing from the rich and giving to the poor. Yep, I thought I was like Robin Hood. With a friend I had met earlier that year, we spent one summer on horseback, stealing from abandoned houses and robbing an antique store and making off with the goods to drop them off down a dirt road where poor people lived. It just made no sense to us that so many of the town people lived well, while a mile down the road people were living in houses with dirt floors and hardly any clothes, never mind nice dishes. We supplied them with a lot of that! Sometimes it would be getting dark when we returned home, so we started stashing our loot in a little shed in the back yard. We had quite a pile of stuff and since my Aunt rarely came out to our little hideout, we figured it was safe there.

One night she showed up and was shocked to see all of the stuff we had. She knew we were stealing and she got really upset and was shouting, "Oh, my God, the High Sheriff is going to come and arrest you both and take you to jail." For those of you that do not know what a High Sheriff is, it is a lawman—the Sheriff that rides a horse. Because you had to look up from the ground to talk to him sitting high upon his horse, the term "High Sheriff" came about.

Anyway, that was the last of our looting because after that, we were terrified about the High Sheriff coming after us, as we were told his horse was faster and we could not outrun him. Thus ended our Robin Hood days.

I believe we are born naturally empathetic, naturally compassionate towards humans and animals.

Negative beliefs, thoughts and feelings are mostly learned. Beliefs can be passed down generation to generation just like genetics. I love to listen to children talk about animals, because their innocence and natural respect and love towards animals is such a beautiful thing to experience. They often know things about animals that we as adults do not always perceive.

The sheer innocence of a child's heart connects them to their deep perception of the world around them. It is through negative experiences that our attention is taken away from that place of innocence. It is through love that we can reconnect and communicate with the animals on a deeper level.

This fast-paced and socially dysfunctional world we live in is creating humans with attention deficit disorders. It is teaching people how *not* to hold their attention on anything for very long. Multi-tasking is the order of the day, along with communicating in text talk language. How hard it has become to "Be still and know..."

Early Horse Communication

I value my childhood experience, as I drew from it when I got older and started my Animal Communication journey. I was about seven, on the farm, when we had company from the city. Among them was a girl a few years older than me that rode horses in the city. I was told I was to let her ride my horse. Before she even arrived, I felt dreadful about the situation (early intuition?) and felt I did not want her on my horse, but southern politeness was pretty darn important in those parts of the country and my aunt insisted that I "behave." The girl was not out of the car but a few minutes when she looked over at me on my horse and asked to ride. I said "No, my horse will not understand you." There was just so much about her I could feel that was, well, just plain not nice. You, the reader, I am sure, have had moments where your intuition speaks so loudly to you that you just have to pay attention. I had never heard of the word intuition or anything like that, but I heard something in my thoughts. They were words very faintly telling me not to let her ride. The adults won and I handed over the reins. My horse was a kind, gentle, tough, solid cow-working horse. We did everything together—jump ditches, swam, rounded up cows. I could put children on him, two people on him at a time—he was what you would refer to back then as "solid broke" and no spook in him at all. She got on him and, as she did, I leaned up to his ear and told him, "Please, for me, throw her off."

She took off galloping out of sight, and a few minutes later, my horse is running back to me with no rider. The adults got in a car and drove about a mile down the road and brought her back. She was not hurt, except her ego, and told us he threw her off. My Aunt grabbed me by the arm and took me out in the back of the house, grabbing a switch on the way. When we got back there she leaned down and looked at me closely in the eyes and asked, "Did you tell your horse to throw her off?" Before I could answer, she said, "I know you did and you know that horse is going to hear you and listen to you don't you?!" I never got a spanking; she let me go. The point is, she believed my horse threw the city girl because I told him to, which made me believe it, too. Nothing quite that close has happened to me with a horse since, but I have heard amazing stories from my clients about their relationship with their horses. They know of which I speak.

> As one of my clients said, "Catherine, I think thoughts to my horse, and then I wait and listen in my heart and mind for what thoughts come back to me from my horse." Exactly! That is it! That is, in essence, the basics of Animal Communication.

Does this mean that animals always do what we tell them to? No, it does not. They have free will, too. But I believe in some human/animal relationships there is more going on than meets the eye. Close relationships often result in spontaneous telepathy, such as when a husband and wife tell you that they finish each other's sentences. It is like they know what the other is thinking and what the other is about to say, and I believe they do. They are linked by their open heart and mind to each other. Usually, you can feel the love they have for each other when they tell you about these experiences. So, on that note, I believe my horse heard me and responded. After all, I was a child with an open heart and mind, and I loved my horse beyond comprehension. It is sad how most of us lose that innocence as we grow older.

Animals are keen at reading a person's energy. They have to be that way, especially horses. To horses, humans are predators. The two-eyed predator making friends with the prey (the horse). How honored I have always felt that I was accepted by any animal as a friend, especially a horse. When I was a child, I was so concerned about horses seeing us humans as predators that I did not like to eat meat. My other best friend was a goat, and people in that part of the country raised goats to eat. I felt like if I ate meat, I was eating my friends. Who eats their friends?

Back to age four. I had a lot of freedom at that age, I think, perhaps more than most little girls. I loved feeling that way, but I only felt it when riding in the woods. I was allowed to ride my horse, Dixie, in the back pasture where we kept our cows, and I loved to go check the fences and check on the cows on horseback. One day, I took off and went far back into the woods so I could ride and be alone. As I was riding through the woods, suddenly a wild turkey took flight directly above Dixie and me, with the wings of the turkey coming so close they brushed my back. I can still recall the rush of feeling of the turkey's feathers over me. As the turkey flew over, the wind felt like it picked up all around me and I heard a voice say, "I am here. Look around you, because I am here." It was a profound experience for me, especially as young as I was. I went back to the farm house and told my Aunt about it. I told her I did not need to go back to the church people again because they would not understand. I also told her I thought I had figured out what was meant by "In my Father's house are many mansions..." And I told her I thought God was in the woods, in the animals, in the trees and just everywhere. She looked at me with exasperation and asked where I got these kinds of thoughts and thinking, but it was more like a statement than a question. I did not know the answer anyway.

An Unexpected Dimensional Visit from My Childhood Horse

Many years later, in the 80's when I was barrel racing, I had a visit from my childhood horse who had long ago passed away. His name was Dan.

I was not into the study of things metaphysical at that time. I was just working, riding my horses and going to barrel races on the weekends. It was fun and I had a couple of fine horses and a great social life with the other barrel racers. By then, I had two horse trainers as my friends and, when I was not working at the hospital, all else was horses. This particular weekend, I was really excited as I was going to a rodeo with a friend. I was not riding in the grand entry parade, but she was so I was watching closely so as to learn the riding pattern. A couple of minutes into the show, as all the horses and riders were parading at a canter in the arena, with the crowd cheering as the beautiful cowgirls displayed their horses, all of a sudden I see a horse in the arena with a saddle, bridle and *no rider*. I thought someone had fallen off their horse, so I ran to the announcer and told him. He looked out into the arena and said he did not see anything like that. I looked again and saw the horse with no rider and then realized what I was seeing looked like, or was, my childhood horse, Dan. I started walking around the stands where the crowds were seated and randomly asking people if they saw a horse with no rider in the grand entry parade. No one did. Only me. When I came back around, I asked the riders in the rodeo if anyone noticed a horse with no rider. None of them did.

What I believe happened that afternoon was that my childhood horse, Dan, briefly made his way through the dimensions and showed himself to me. It was a visit from another "mansion." It was a message that brought my senses back to the way I saw and experienced life as a child. Thus, it was the real beginning of my adult experiences, or awareness, and what I learned from it was that those other mansions and worlds might reveal themselves to us, but the most important to me was *the message that there is no death.*

I shared this experience with some of my friends. I got questioned:

Are you taking any medication?

Were you drinking?

Are you schizophrenic?

I learned to keep my experiences to myself!

Now, 20 years later, I have lost the fear of being concerned with what people think of me. I guess it is one of the perks of getting older. I just lost the feeling of being worried about other people around me being comfortable with who I am, but a lot of that was due to the ongoing experiences and the stories my patients in the hospital were sharing with me about seeing their loved ones who had died, along with my horse clients telling me similar stories. And, of course, the visits I personally had from the ones who have passed from this earth. At this point in my life, I have given hundreds of consults and been extensively interviewed by the media. I found a way to deal with the grief in my life and it was, and still is, by helping someone or an animal when I can. What else could we be here on this planet for? An elderly lady once told me, "We are not here to see through each other, but rather to see each other through."

There Is No Death

I was working in the emergency room when an elderly woman (she was 94) was brought in. As I was working with her, I felt an intuitive urge (happens often) to ask her more about herself. She told me her husband had passed away about 10 years before and how she had been grieving since. She said they met when they were children, grew up together in a small southern town and were inseparable. I asked if she ever had any dreams about him that seemed very real to her. She said, "Oh, my, yes, I do. Pretty often I wake up in the middle of the night and see him at my bedside! He looks younger and smiles at me." She continued, "I don't tell many people about that because they will think I made it up or that I am a crazy old woman."

But perhaps the part of her story that made such a huge difference in my thinking was this:

The rabbit did not die.

The story went that when she and her husband were young, he took her rabbit hunting. Seeing a rabbit fleeing through the woods, her husband shot and killed the rabbit. She was watching it all and she said that as soon as the rabbit was hit with a bullet she saw the rabbit drop to the ground, but also saw it continue running away in what appeared to be a bright yellow and white light body. She could still tell it was the rabbit, but it was glowing with yellow and white colors that seemed transparent. Her husband picked up the physical body of the rabbit he shot, but she had clearly seen the energy body of the rabbit leave. She said she realized then that there was so much more to this world than what we thought. She never told her husband, but she told me. After that, she said she never ate meat again and from that time on she had a completely different belief about life. She said that belief was, *"there is no death."* Then she looked at me and said, "Well, after all it is even in the Bible—in my Father's house are many mansions..." She had never heard me say that, and I smiled and hugged her and told her I believed every word of her story.

The terms energy body, light body, electronic body, and ethereal body are all interchangeable. They all refer to the body following physical death. The terms dimensions and mansions are interchangeable also, in this book. They refer to the various realms of existence we experience. We are interdimensional beings. There are so many aspects of ourselves and the animals, but in our culture we focus mostly on our physical existence. Accessing these other dimensions takes dedicated work with meditation and a balance in living life in the physical realm. Sometimes, I am so inside myself thinking and feeling on these other dimensional levels, I will walk right into a tree! It takes some discipline to keep one foot in the spiritual realms and one in the physical. Such as when I am riding my horse,

I must keep us both physically safe, and of course that starts with paying attention!

I did not discuss these experiences often, for many reasons. First, I didn't share what I consider sacred experiences with just anyone, which made writing this book very difficult. I wrote it because I have been giving this information in lectures to special groups of people, such as at the Chapel of Spiritual Light in Orlando, Florida, and also sharing privately with some of my clients over the years. I realized it was time to share and it is in that Light that I write most humbly.

Sam Speaks About a Visit from Another Dimension

As a Respiratory Therapist in a rehabilitation hospital, I had a patient about 55 years old named Sam. He was there for rehabilitation following an accident, doing very well relearning to walk following injury to his knees. Cognitively, he was fine. He always made my day with his smiles and sense of humor. One morning I went in his room, as I often did, to say hello. As I walked in, Sam was talking to someone I could not see. I stood and listened and his last words spoken to the unseen guest were, "I will see you soon." It was then that I walked up close to him and asked him what was going on. I said, "Sam, I do not see anyone in this room. What is happening?" He responded with, "Cathy, that was my wife who died a couple of years ago. She came to see me, and she told me I would be joining her soon." Sam had never had any experience like this, but he did tell me that the last few nights he had felt someone sitting on his bed. He would open his eyes and no one was there. Then, that morning, he saw and was talking with his deceased wife. Sam and I carried on quite a conversation about this and it crossed my mind to notify the on-call psychologist, but when I asked Sam about doing that he told me to please not to. Sam was ready to be discharged home in less than a week. Three days later, I went to work and was told he had passed away quietly in the night.

I have hundreds of stories like this from my patients in the span of the 35 years I have worked in the medical field. There is a common theme between all of them. Many of them tell me they just woke up in the middle of the night and experienced a visit from a loved one who had died. Some of them describe it as a dream, but all of them say the visit brought them great peace regarding the afterlife.

A Visit from Dano, a Transition into the Light

Dano was my life partner and we had been together many years. I got the dreaded phone call at 3 a.m. one morning that he was in the Intensive Care Unit following a car accident. He often worked late and was on his way home when the accident happened. He was thrown from his truck and was without oxygen until medics arrived and he was too long without oxygen. He also suffered head trauma and many fractured bones.

I left immediately for the hospital to find him hooked up to life support equipment and with a tracheotomy in place for breathing. The physician came in and showed me the reports from his test, showing he was, in layman's terms, "brain dead." No sign of normal activity on his EEG test. Having worked the Intensive Care Unit as a Respiratory Therapist, I knew what all of this meant.

I came home and crawled in bed. I was so exhausted, I did not meditate that night and I drifted off to sleep, still numb and in shock. I don't remember what time it was, but I woke up with a strange feeling and there, by my bed, was Dano. He was covered in blood and very upset, asking me, "Where am I? What happened to me?" I was in shock at seeing him. His body looked very physical. I did not touch him to see.

It was something I had never experienced and I was not quite sure if I was having a nightmare or if this was real. I sat up and I spoke out loud telling him he was in an accident and that his body was in the Intensive Care Unit. He listened and then he disappeared like in a cloud of smoke. Gone.

I got dressed and went back to the hospital and sat with him there, talking to him, and stroking his hands. He was and had been in a coma in the hospital since the accident. So, who, what was it that visited me at home? My belief is it was him in the form of an electronic body, an energy body, an ethereal body or body of Light as I have heard it called. Just like the rabbit.

Energy cannot be destroyed, it can only be transformed. The first law of thermodynamics, also known as Law of Conservation of Energy, states that energy can neither be created nor destroyed; energy can only be transferred or changed from one form to another.

Or in other words, changed from one form to another— *transformed!*

Dano was in between worlds. To me, he was in one of the *mansions*, one of the dimensions of our existence while making his ascension, or transition, into the Heavenly Realms of Light.

Then another visit occurred. This time, I was just drifting off to sleep and he appeared. Looking much younger and healed from the car accident, he communicated with me that he understood what had happened. He told me he was sorry he had to leave me. Then, poof, he was gone. It was like he dissipated in a cloud of vapor. I went back to sleep and visited him again in the morning. He was transferred to a hospice house as the family and I had decided it was time to let him go, meaning withdraw any treatment except comfort measures.

Dano and I had discussed our wishes previously should anything of this nature ever happen to either one of us. But having him visit me in his energy body and communicate with me, I knew, without a doubt, this was his choice.

The third night he visited again. This time, things were most different. He was smiling, even laughing. He had a guitar in his hand (he was an accomplished musician). He was beaming with bright, glowing yellow and white light and told me he would not be back but that he would be watching over me. He told me he loved me and all would be okay. Then he disappeared, vanished in a vapor of light energy. Gone from my physical sight.

I never saw him again in a visit. Meanwhile, his physical body was still in the hospice house. When I went there to see him, as soon as I walked in the door I could feel his spirit was gone. What was before me was just a physical body. Dano had made his transition into the Light and I knew it.

Years later, an old high school friend of mine contacted me. We got together and he came out to my place. Seeing all the things that needed fixing, he said he wanted to help me be more comfortable. Like Dano, he was a master with woodworking and fixing things. One day, when he was here working, he walked through my back door and called me by the name Dano called me— a pet name that only close family and friends ever heard. When he said it, I turned in disbelief and then he followed up with, "I don't know why I just called you that name, huh."

Of course, I knew and I told him about it being Dano's pet name for me. "Hmmm," he said, "looks like he is speaking to me to look out for you!" And so, it is. Dano told me he would be looking out for me in our last visit.

We just never know who is whispering to us from dimensions beyond our physical sight. This is one of the reasons when I meditate, I pray for protection. I ask to be lifted up beyond and above this earthly plane and into the realms of Light, into the Mansion of Heaven.

Why does it seem they always disappear in a cloud of vapor?

My thoughts on this are that the reason the visits end may not always be that the person or animal leaves, as it seems they disappear in a cloud of smoke or vapor, but it may be that I am not able to keep myself in that state of awareness any longer and access the other dimensions. They always seem to happen when I am in between the sleep and awake state.

It seems the more I wake up to this world we live in, this physical world, I lose the connection with the other dimension, the spirit world.

Visit from a Guardian Angel and Something Else

In 1996, when I started my Animal Communication consults, I was also attending classes in Mediumship at the famous Cassadaga Spiritualist Camp Association. My teacher was the Rev. Jerry Frederich, a former pastor of the Colby Memorial Temple. I was still working at a hospital where I was on call and stayed at the facility two nights in a row, mainly on call for the emergency room. As a Respiratory Therapist, my job was first in line in a Code Blue to provide the patients an airway. This means establish a way for a patient to breathe. It is a high stress job, as you can imagine.

At this time, after learning to meditate, I practiced every day. One night at the hospital when I was on call, I lay down on the uncomfortable hospital bed in my cold, bleak call room and I began to meditate. This time, I first sat on the bed, eyes closed, breathing deeply, I asked, "Father/Mother God, lift my consciousness out of this world and into the other dimensions, the other mansions, so I can learn more. Allow me to see and communicate with my guardian angel." I kept breathing deeply and asking this in my thoughts. I remember lying down on my side and I remember starting to drift to sleep, but something happened. I opened my eyes just slightly. It was as though I was in limbo somewhere, half asleep and half awake, and next to my bed, standing very tall with arms stretched out over

Sell your books at sellbackyourBook.com!

Go to sellbackyourBook.com and get an instant price quote. We even pay the shipping - see what your old books are worth today!

Inspected By:soleil

00001614374

00001614374

me, was an angelic being. That is the only way I know how to describe this presence. The being was glowing with golden light. It appeared as though the glowing arms were surrounding me.

I looked down at the foot of my bed and there was the most grotesque being I had ever seen. It was about three feet tall with large eyes. The feeling I got from the experience is that my prayer was answered. I was seeing a Protector, my guardian angel. I was also seeing the interdimensional beings that we might need protection from. The angel did not speak. I believe I was in shock and the more I woke up, the less I could see this magnificent angel.

It changed my life forever. I have never felt the same nor have I looked at life the way I used to. I believe. Two important factors here: one, I had been, and still am on, a quest for contact with the realms of Light, the angels; and two, I did not give up. I kept at this meditation and, lo and behold, I got an answer.

The next morning, I called my Grandmother from the payphone in the hospital lobby. She was a deeply spiritual lady. I was able to share this part of my life with her because she had similar experiences all of her life. She was a Southern Baptist and charter member of her church, a highly respected true southern lady with a brilliant recall of poems and Bible verses. When I shared this story about the visit from the angel I could hear the excitement in her voice, the excitement as she told me she had the same experience a few nights before.

But hers was minus the little nasty being at the foot of the bed. I told her that was probably because she had lived such a sacred life and mine had been pretty darn colorful. She chuckled at that. She was so happy that she had someone who understood her experiences, and I was grateful for her believing and supporting mine.

My background in college was in science, of course. I was always seeking an explanation for these experiences. One thing that became very clear to me was:

- I was seeking, I was asking. "Ask and you shall receive."
- I was living as close to Nature as possible. In my free time, I was outside learning to work with horses.
- I spent little time around people and I practiced, stayed tuned in to my inner guidance.
- I paid attention to details and, if a bird flew across my path, I would be listening for any messages from that bird.
- I found little value in small talk and most social gatherings. Loud people and unnatural sounds really bothered me.
- I loved meditating and listening to beautiful music and found peace in being alone or with the horses.

- I started to explore the idea that the Kingdom of Heaven really is within, if I could only learn to stay there!
- I started watching my thoughts and when I found my mind was too busy with just stuff, I would calm it down through meditation and remind myself that those inner thoughts must be brought under control.

Meditation

Life led me to a friendship with a medical doctor who also studied hypnosis. I learned a lot about the human brain from him. Some of the information he gave me was about brainwave patterns. It is said that the Alpha state is the one most often connected to meditation and hypnosis. The Beta state is where we are most alert and most active. Meditation affects your brain waves. For me, being somewhat scientific, it helped to see the importance of meditation.

I venture to say the visits from those that have passed have occurred while in the Alpha state. I believe we can train our minds to be in that state even when wide awake. When I would talk about "lifting up in consciousness into the other realms and dimensions of life" my physician friend would talk in scientific terms, of entering Alpha states. Nonetheless, we were on the same page, just different perspectives of where we were going with it. I started using this theory with meditation and taking notice when I had entered another state of consciousness. There were, and still are, times when it is difficult for me to hold my attention on being in a meditative state because the pull, like gravity, sucks me back into a linear, more earth-bound state of mind and the connection disappears.

So I have learned it is a commitment, it takes time and training oneself with a deep heartfelt yearning to know. Because of this heartfelt commitment, it has changed me in many ways and the things that were once seemingly so important to me, are not anymore.

I also studied deeply the teachings from eraofpeace.org. For a few years, my experiences took me to the famous Cassadaga Spiritualist Camp Association in Cassadaga, Florida, where I studied Healing and Mediumship for a while, but lost interest in working with people in that way. My heart had always been with the animal kingdom. During those years, I was driving from Tallahassee to Cassadaga, a four-and-a-half-hour one-way trip for me, just to attend class once a week. Often, I had to return the next day as I was working in a hospital almost full time. This is what I mean by being committed. I learned a lot that helped me on my journey, and I made lifelong friends with other spiritually minded people. I think I was beyond committed, more like desperate to discover these other dimensions of existence for my own soul's peace.

Grief and Visits from Nina, My Canine Best Friend

During the period of Nina's illness (she had a disease commonly referred to as Lar Par, a breathing disorder), I knew our time together was coming to an end. She had been with me since she was a puppy and she was 14 when she passed. I was already grieving over the thought of being without her. Every moment with her seemed precious and I did not want to leave the house for anything without her being with me. Going to work became harder and harder. I began to resent absolutely anything or anyone that took away from my time with Nina. Lar Par is a horrible way to die. Being a Respiratory Therapist, I have sadly watched people die from breathing disorders. It is horrifying to watch people struggle to breathe.

Nina's first attack of this dreadful disease landed us in an animal emergency clinic in the middle of the night. The kind and intelligent vet on call diagnosed her. We x-rayed her chest also and found a tumor on her heart. Her days were numbered, I was told, so I took her home with medicine to keep her comfortable. Three weeks later, she had another attack. I medicated her to calm her down then took her the next morning to be euthanized at my regular vet's office. No more of this. I was not going to put her through suffering and struggling to breathe. I did not discuss this decision with anyone with the exception of the emergency room veterinarian, in which I simply asked her, "If this were your best friend, what would you do?" Her answer swayed my decision.

The first night after Nina had been euthanized; I was in my bed crying. It seemed like my crying would not stop even long enough for me to take a breath or drink any water. I held my own body trying to comfort it. As my dear friend, Dr. Richard Powers (healthcoachdoctor. com), said, "The crying, the grief comes in waves. If it did not come in waves, I do not know if one would be able to bear it."

I cried until I was choking, my bed wet with tears. Sometime during the night, I drifted off to sleep. I don't recall how long it was, but sometime during the night, I woke up and I saw Nina's face close to me. Just like with Dano, she was questioning me. She did not know what had happened.

From this I learned how important it is to actually tell an animal what is going on. We should help them transcend to the next world. I realized that when she was euthanized I did not communicate clearly with her about what was happening. I was too caught up in my own pain and feelings of loss.

So there I was, Nina, just like Dano, had come to me. I sat up in bed, the tears pouring out again, and I told Nina out loud that she was very sick and that she had entered a different world now. And, just like with Dano, poof, she disappeared in a cloud vapor-like substance of light.

My second day without her was just as hard, and the waves of grief, as Dr. Powers described, seemed to come faster and harder. I was thinking of the last time I visited Destin Beach in Florida, and how I was being knocked about by the waves. Each time I would stand up in just three feet of water, another wave would come and knock me off my balance and back under the water. That is how it felt, maybe a few seconds before another wave hit.

That is what grief feels like to me—hardly a reprieve. Hardly time to catch my breath before being thrown about again, never ending stormy high waves with no relief. There was nothing to soothe or comfort me, only feelings of loss, displacement and sadness. Thoughts of suicide entered my mind often. If I could just go where Nina was, but I knew that was not an option as I knew there were no guarantees I would end up in the same dimension or same place. I knew I truly did not want to die, but I also did not know how to live here on planet Earth without Nina. The truth is, I did not know how to go about my life anymore without her.

The second night after her passing away, she visited again. And again, like with Dano, she appeared and looked younger and she seemed happy. There was little communication that night, it was more visual. It brought me peace, and it was like she knew she was moving on from this world and was saying goodbye to me for now.

The third night, she appeared to me glowing in an energy-like substance, what I call the energy body or light body or electronic body, as I described earlier. She smiled her Nina dog smile and was looking at me with her usual looks of adoration. Then, she was gone. She had made her ascension, her transition from the earth plane of existence into the realms of Light. She disappeared in a cloud of Light. I have not seen or heard from her since. Her visits brought me peace and slowly I started to heal. But the missing her here with me has never gone away, and I have to stop at times and consciously remember her visits to remind myself that she really is okay. It is just me that is not "okay" at times, because I miss her physically. But it pushes me, forces me, to continue my meditations and quest to be allowed to enter these other dimensions, permission to access them.

Pursuing this life is a challenge, there is work—keeping money coming in. Taking care of myself and my other animals and just plain life.

Kyla's Transition without Visits

My dog Kyla passed away a short time before Nina. She was about 15 years old and had been sick the previous year. She was just growing old and getting to the end of her doggie life. During the day, while I was at work, she stayed outside when the weather was good, in her little dog house and large pen. The day she passed away, I was at work and suddenly I was filled with overwhelming emotion and sadness. My thoughts turned to Kyla. I knew she needed me and I immediately came up with some excuse for leaving work. As many of you already know, some of the time an employer will not sympathize with your concerns about your sick dog; therefore, I think I told them I was so sick to my stomach I had to leave.

I made it home just in time to find Kyla taking her last breaths. I picked her up and held her as she passed away, talking to her, telling her how much I loved her. Telling her, between tears, how much I appreciated it that she picked me to live her life with. She left this world peacefully in my arms. I was alone with Kyla. There were many people I could have called, but I was frozen, I could hardly move. I remember I was standing up holding her and made my way to the ground with her still in my arms. Finally, I called my son's phone number and he came right out. I was still crying when he got here. I made him check and double check that she was really physically dead. We buried her and her grave is marked with her toys.

I never heard from nor have I seen Kyla again. Not in my dreams or any telepathic communication, intuition or any visitations at all. I prayed to her to come see me, but nothing ever happened. It was like Kyla just vanished from all dimensions. But I believe she didn't. I believe Kyla was not as earth bound as Nina was. Kyla always had one ear tuned to the call of the wild and I believe that when she realized she no longer had an earth body, she took off running just like the rabbit in the story I told you. She was free, and just as in earth life, Kyla loved her freedom. Knowing that, I am more at peace with Kyla's passing.

I do not believe we or our animals change a lot when we make this transition called death. Most of us now know we are here on this planet to learn and to love. It does not make any real sense in the natural order of things that suddenly we would just change our personality when we make this transition from earthly body to the energy body. Perhaps in some cases we do. That I do not know. I am only discussing here what I have directly experienced, but I definitely believe we live on in another dimension, or mansion. Perhaps there we continue our learning experiences, and perhaps there, some are ordained as angels to look out for us from the Heavenly realms!

My Mother: A Difficult Visit

Without going into detail, because I have family that feels differently and I wish not to cause any problems, it is enough to say that my biological mother and I fought probably from the time I was born. I never really got along with her. There seemed nothing I could do that would ever please her. Of course, I realize I am the only person to ever have a bad relationship with her or his mother!

As I got older, and hopefully wiser, I started to realize that she was probably doing the best she could. When you are a child, you do not know that. I still often have to be disciplined enough to switch my attention back to the truth, the truth that most people are doing the best they can. She passed away a few years ago, her illness long and difficult on her and my family. I was there when I could be and helped when I could. The reason I share this deeply personal and private information is because of what happened after she passed away.

That night I woke up, once again feeling a presence in my room, and there she was pretty much in my face, yelling at me. She was saying negative things to me as she would sometimes do in earthly life. She was criticizing me from the other side! It made me cry; it scared me. I always thought maybe she would be kinder and gentler to me when she made her transition.

It happened again the second night.

The third night, I did a meditation that evening and specifically prayed to God for protection, and then I said a prayer to my mother as I was wondering if she would ever leave me alone. I think I was secretly hoping she would communicate something loving to me. Finally, on that night, I saw her again and this time she looked young. She was sitting at a table, like at a luncheon, and was talking with a group of friends. She was smiling and laughing. The people around her appeared to be medical professionals and they were talking about neurology, an area of interest to her. In life, my mother was a RN, and a brilliant woman. I believe that she made her transition and found others with whom she felt happy and shared a common interest. I never saw her again. I believe she is at peace, and I am, too.

By now, you may have noticed a common theme that I have become aware of in all my experiences when a human or an animal passes away—the time from physical death to transition into the other realms of Light, has been three days. This is significant enough for me that, when someone passes now, I am on alert for visits and messages from them and consider the next three days as a holy and sacred time.

Once they have transitioned into those other higher dimensions, we may lose physical sight of them. I think until we learn how to connect to the other realms and remain there long enough, they will remain out of our physical ability to see them. However, having said that, I also believe because of my own experiences, this could change. It has been said by other seers that the veils between our worlds are growing thinner and that we are moving into higher dimensions. How grand it would be, to be united in Life with those now in Spirit, right in the here and now!

Grief

Grief is experienced differently by each person. Every person is unique and will experience grief in his or her own personal way. This is vitally important to know for yourself and for those you may be assisting while they experience the loss of a loved one. Think of how we all have different fingerprints, then think of our souls as all being just as different. As a Spiritualist, I intellectually know there is no death. I know this, however, only because of my own experiences and visits from my loved ones who have passed away, and not because someone told me it was true or because I read it somewhere. But it does not make the experience of losing a loved one any less painful. The truth is, we would give anything for one more hug from the ones we love, and that is a very physical thing. The apparent absence of those we love, because we can no longer see, hear, or interact with them in our daily lives, is a profound loss. Mine, and others I have witnessed, resulted in an emotional breakdown.

What is a breakdown and how does it feel? For me, my central nervous system went into overload from trying to deal with the grief, work, and maintain my home and other animals. My mind was scattered, I had trouble forming complete sentences, I could not stay on task to finish anything, and I did not care or remember at times if I had taken a bath. Food was a hassle and I ate mostly fast food because I did not want to cook, since that reminded me too much of Nina and Kyla as we usually ate at the same time. I would burst out crying often. The worst of it was the dread I felt being inside buildings, grocery stores or away from home for any reason. You know how dogs often circle around before they lie down? Well, I felt like I was in a permanent state of circling. No place felt safe, comfortable or peaceful enough to stop and lie down. Also, I wanted to meditate and ask for permission to enter the other dimensions; however, my grief was so overwhelming, I could not calm myself down long enough to meditate and pray. I wondered if it would ever end.

I sought help. I found a grief counselor.

My counselor coached me through getting my balance back. When I first went in to see her, I could barely hold any papers in my hand. I was shaking most of the time. Just the drive from my place in the country into the city triggered my grief and some level of post-traumatic stress. I have always considered myself a strong and independent woman, so I had to battle judging myself, thinking of myself as weak, because I needed help. After all, I was always the one there for other people. How could I be this messed up?

Then I remembered, "Grief is lodged in the body." Now I was getting it. Now I was starting to understand why it would not just get better on its own, and I was remembering what I went through and wrote about years ago. I want to share here what I wrote back then and presented at one of my workshops. I was so depressed and sad *I had forgotten my own words of understanding that I had shared years ago*. That is what grief does to you. You lose touch with everything except the grief itself. Grief becomes a place, like a house you live in, and it is damn hard to move out of it.

When an Animal Dies

Lecture at the Animal Communication Workshop in Cassadaga, FL

This article is not a substitute for counseling. My personal experiences over the years with my animal friends and with my human patients and friends has given me some insights that I am sharing in the spirit of helping others.

We hear so often following the death of an animal friend that they have "gone to the Light or crossed over the Rainbow Bridge," so much that the mere sound of those words leaves us possibly accepting those truths or in a state of confusion. We hear from others that "they live on." But where? We may even solicit the services of a Medium to communicate with our deceased loved one for us. But how do we really know they live in another realm without us having the direct personal experience, direct personal contact?

It might be difficult at first for our mentally oriented minds to fathom some of the things I talk about; however, as we open up to other aspects of ourselves, other possibilities that exist within us, we can come to understand that what is sometimes described as Psychic, ESP or Mediumship is actually our natural evolution and is normal. We come to understand that often purely mentally thinking about something can be limiting. When we open our hearts through love and meditation, we can discover for ourselves and we can come into a closer relationship with those aspects of ourselves that harbor a deep inner knowing about life. Our dreams become more real, our thoughts become more important than spoken language; our feelings become a system we rely on more than what is being told or said to us. In other words, it is from our open hearts that we communicate with our loved ones who have passed from this earthly plane of existence. We simply need to learn to trust what comes to us in our thoughts and feelings, dreams and visions.

Telepathy is open heart and mind communication. It is communication through thoughts, feelings and images. It is using our deepest empathy to connect with an animal or person. It is our God-given ability that we have lost touch with. But it is there waiting for us, *if we turn our attention to it*.

In our culture it seems we are mainly focused on the physical. How we look, what kind of vehicle we drive and... shopping. Yet one of our greatest fears and our greatest sadness is the experience of the death of loved ones. Depending on our background and belief system, we either fear it more and more as we grow older, or we are waiting until our own death to be reunited with our loved ones. Do we really have to wait until we die, physically leave the earth, to reunite with our loved ones?

Do we need someone to make the connection for us? I don't think so. If an average person like me can learn to access the realms and other dimensions, then so can you. That is why I no longer give consults for animals that have crossed over. I will guide the person through the process so can they experience it as I have, if they ask—this way they can know for themselves the truth.

It is up to them to turn their attention to it and learn it.

But it is more than that. It is about what you put first in life. What is a priority in life for you? Is your spiritual growth first? If not, what is? It is what you are putting your attention on in your life. At any given moment, we can choose out of millions of possibilities of where to place our attention! Where is your attention most of the time?

When I started this journey, I started it because I have always wondered what kind of God would create humans and leave them without the ability to communicate with those they love! What could possibly be worse than to lose those you care about? Nothing I could think of. Working in the emergency room and intensive care unit was heartbreaking. So much death. There had to be a way.

The more I could quiet my mind through meditation and horseback riding, the more I could hear my inner voice. The more time I spent in nature, the more I started to perceive energies and visually see energy fields around trees, rocks, animals and people. Connecting with other people who were also experiencing these things was a huge relief and help. I have had many teachers who have helped me on this journey, a journey I am still on. I am humbled by the people who took the time to discuss these matters with me, share with me and encourage me. Especially my patients who opened up and told me beautiful stories of communication with their loved ones who had passed on.

For now, many years later, there are many of us and we can now be found in many mainstream areas of the workforce. Especially needed in hospitals is the kind nurse who listens to dying patients, who is empathic enough to hear their stories and look not in disbelief when they tell you they see someone who has passed away now sitting on their bed with them. I know some nurses like that and they truly might be angels in disguise! They are often referred to as "Lightworkers."

There are already a lot of people who have experienced visitations, who now know that the electronic energy body of light lives on. It will change our views about death; it will help heal the sorrow.

But what about us? We are left in this lower dimension of Earth with this haunting, hurting and devastating condition called grief. This is the story I shared in a newsletter and I have learned a lot since but I think it has value today. While sharing this at my workshop I performed kinesiology on one of the students who had just lost her dog. Kinesiology is a form of muscle testing that many healthcare people use. In fact, my chiropractor performs it on me. You place your fingers on the arm of the other person, I have them close their eyes, and then I put various objects or substances in their other hand. When I press my fingers on their arm, after having told them to try to force my fingers up, their body will usually weaken, their arm drops if the substance is something not good for them. It will test strong with healthy things in their hand. It is an interesting thing to observe. My body tests weak with a watch on. The energy of the watch affects my energy body. I cannot sleep with electronics plugged in near the head of my bed. I feel drained if I do. At the workshop, as soon as we sat my dog Kyla next to the student, her body went from weak to strong. She felt it. She had her eyes closed and did not know Kyla was standing next to her, so when she opened her eyes, she was amazed at the difference she felt with an animal next to her, in her personal or energy field, as I often refer to it as.

Mary's Story

Mary was in her early thirties, worked full time and lived alone with Brandy, her canine companion of ten years. Brandy was her best friend and the one she looked forward to seeing every day when she came home from a less than satisfactory job. Her friends, family, and boyfriend all said that she loved Brandy more than anyone. It was no surprise to them that when Brandy died Mary became depressed. What they could not understand was why Mary continued to be depressed and often locked herself in her house, not wanting to see anyone, not wanting to go to work or do anything social. She found me through a mutual friend and asked to see me. When she finally came to my house, she had lost weight and was barely able to speak about Brandy; her tears were endless. About all she could get out to vocalize to me was, "I can't go on. I can't feel. I am lost. Part of me feels like it is missing."

Having recently been through the death of my beloved dog, PSA, I was seeing in Mary a mirror image of myself in her response to Brandy's death. As I looked at Mary, I knew down to the depths of my soul the pain and feelings of loss that are difficult to express to those around you. Everyone thought she should "be over it" and "go back to work." As I listened to her, I could see her energy, her auric field, and it was like there was a hole in it. The energies were swirling around, not whole. When an animal dies, it literally does take a piece of us with them. It actually leaves a void in us. We don't know how to fill it, and that is why it feels like we are torn apart. We are. I told Mary that I could "see her hurt." I acknowledged or put into words how she felt. I could see relief on her face, because apparently she had not talked to someone who had experienced this level of grief.

I gave her a glass of water. In the grief state, the body can easily become dehydrated due to the stress. Many people do not eat or drink properly during this time;

they simply can't. I also asked her if she could go see her family doctor and discuss obtaining an excuse to be out of work longer. Just that in itself helped Mary, because finally someone understood just how bad she felt. She agreed she could do that. Remember, she was being told by the people around her to "just get over it."

Then I asked her if I could perform kinesiology on her. I explained to her what it was and she agreed. I put several things in her hand such as sugar and she tested weak. She had her eyes closed, so she could not see what all I tested her with. I had little packets of several things I use for this. After a few times of testing her, I quietly cued my dog Kyla to come and sit beside Mary. Kyla pretty much tiptoed over. Mary's eyes were still closed. I tested her with Kyla there and she tested strong! I told her to open her eyes and look down. When she saw Kyla, she smiled for the first time and reached down and hugged Kyla. Mary told me that while she was standing there with her eyes closed, she suddenly felt stronger. I was as amazed as Mary was. I was seeing and learning a whole lot about grief and what it does to the body.

The love she shared with Brandy was still alive. After all, love is an energy that cannot be destroyed. Mary said it was helpful that she was able to identify the loss and understand the way she was feeling. It validated her feelings without me saying much at all. She experienced the cause. Her dog was gone from this world. It left a gap and that gap could only be filled by the love she has for animals. That is why no matter how much her family hugged her and tried to comfort her, it just did not help.

I want to be very clear here when I say how upset I feel when people tell others, "Oh, just go get another dog." That is because they think just any dog can replace the one the grieving person lost. It is extremely important that the person in grief makes that decision entirely on their own; leastwise, they be left feeling empty and hollow with a new dog they do not bond with.

But at this time, it felt right for me to say, "Mary, people like us have a special bond with animals. Other people may never understand, and let us not waste our energy on trying to get them to. But, Mary, you have a gift I do not think you are aware of—you are able to love at an incredible level, an extraordinary level of giving and understanding." I did not know Mary well enough to talk with her about communicating with Brandy though prayers, so I did not open that door.

Mary started asking me questions about Kyla, and I told her that all my dogs were once homeless puppies that I found, or that found me. And then, before I could think, these words just flew out of my mouth. I said, "Part of my own grief is that there are about four million animals in shelters, and millions that are euthanized each year."

As soon as I said it, Mary jumped up off my couch and said, "I am heading to an animal shelter right now!" She was gone so fast I could not believe it. I was even afraid I said the wrong thing to her. I did not hear from her for about two months, and then one day she calls me and tells me that she went to an animal shelter. She said she was talking to Brandy in her thoughts as she walked through the shelter. She said she asked Brandy to lead her to the right dog to give a home to and one that would love her. She mailed me a photo of herself and a precious puppy. She said, "Brandy led me to this one."

The story had the happiest ending. I learn so much from the people I meet. I saw so much of the way I feel in Mary and, I think, the way many of us feel.

How to Help Friends Who Are Grieving the Loss of an Animal Companion

Visit them and bring your dog if possible. Your dog can help just by being present (as long as they are well behaved!)

Offer and encourage them to drink water. Bring some special bottled water or tea. Stress can cause dehydration.

Take them food that is easy to warm up. Often people won't eat during this time and they need for food to be simple.

If they have other animals at home, gently remind them that the other animals may be grieving, also. I was amazed that when my beloved dog PSA passed, Kyla and my horse both turned down food that evening.

Support them in taking off work.

Explain to them that their mate may not know what to do to comfort them and may feel frustrated and that this is normal. Mates usually love us so much and want to try to "fix" it for us and they can't.

Encourage them to find refuge perhaps with a grief counselor and certainly with their friends that understand.

My Personal Experiences with Grief

The passing away of an animal friend is often a life changing event. Life will never be the same again. This means relationships with people may change; some may come to an end.

This is because the way you view the world is now different. It is different because you no longer have your animal companion with you and, therefore, your daily life is different. What do you do *now* with that time when you fed your animal, took him/her for a walk, crawled in bed with him/her, and played? There is a huge void. You get up in the morning and reach for your animal's feed bowl, only to realize they are not there. Life becomes so different that it changes you. This is hard on the humans around us. They do not know what we are experiencing and they want things to just go back to the way they were. They want you to be the way you were. Sometimes mates will actually feel jealous of the attention we are giving to our feelings of loss! It happens often. Sometimes we might feel resentful of people we once loved, because they are interfering with our need to grieve, to cry, and be alone to process our feelings. Sometimes people close to us may even become angry at us because we are sad.

Some people have said to be mindful of crying, because the animal, in spirit, can feel you are hurting and it might make them sad, but our human ability to shed tears is a way for our bodies to express the loss. Don't fight it. It is normal and natural, and sometimes that very deep grieving is a ray of energy to help you connect in spirit with your beloved animal friend. Grief drives you ever so deep within yourself, and spontaneous connections with this other mansion in the Light, can occur naturally, on their own. That is because your heart is crying out to God, as you know God.

As I said earlier, the first three days are important to pay attention to what you receive in dreams. This seems to be a time, in my personal experiences, where the animal is making the transition into the Light. If you do not receive any information that does not mean it is not happening. Some of my friends have described that in the first few days they noticed odd things happening with electronics. Things such as a radio just coming on with a particular song that was special to them. Remember, when an animal, or person leaves the physical earth, it is energy, and this energy has the ability to affect many things and, of course, us.

We are also in a state of heightened sensitivity following a death; therefore, we might perceive things that we would otherwise not even notice. We may not have ever paid much attention to our dreams before, and suddenly we do. We may not have considered life following death before, and now we do. These are some of the ways we change, we become different on the inside, and this difference is what often causes our personal relationships with humans to change.

We live on this Earth in a very, very physical existence. So, to me, it only makes sense that I devote my time and energies into searching for answers and understanding this process known as death.

This means I do not live a traditional life. I simply can't if I want to find out these answers. For example, sleep has become extremely important to me. Remembering my dreams each morning is imperative. I lie in bed after I wake up, just so I can remember. I ask the Great Spirit for permission to enter the realms and dimensions, as a knowledge seeker, for answers to some of life's greatest mysteries and especially the process of death. I do this through quiet contemplation, prayer and deep breathing. I have to work at keeping my mind still and free of earthly thoughts.

I have an imagery I do—I picture in my mind's eye a tiny angel that has a spear she carries. She hangs around me especially when I am meditating and praying and if any thought tries to enter that is not in line with my prayers, she spears it and takes it into a bright light! She simply takes it away. It works for me, but it took practice to quiet my mind. As I am breathing, I ask to be taken to those places, those dimensions, into the Light.

My Simple Prayer

Father/Mother God, Great Spirit that connects all things, I humbly ask for permission to be taken into the Octaves of Truth, I ask to be allowed into the Kingdom of Heaven, right here and now, inside me.

I am breathing deeply and relaxing. I take notice of what colors I see with my eyes closed. At first, when I started it was all dark, and slowly I began to notice a clearing and then lights. I continue to breathe deeply.

I come before the Angels of Light and ask for Divine Protection from anything that is not of the Light. In this sacred place I ask for permission to communicate with my loved one who has crossed over into the realms of

Light (and I name that animal or person).

Then I wait. I continue to breathe deeply and I listen with my entire being, paying attention to the images I see with my eyes closed and the thoughts that come to me. This is a very sacred and holy place. I don't ask about any earth bound situations. I focus only on the love I have for the animal or person I am missing.

The listening part is so important, and this prayer can take some time.

The first few times I did it, nothing happened. It was like I had to build a relationship with the other side, form a relationship with the angels. That made perfect sense to me; relationships have to be built! Perhaps they needed to know my sincerity, so I did not give up. I had a set time each night to do this meditation.

There are sometimes other blocks. I wrote the following meditation for the audience in Cassadaga, where many Mediums and spiritually minded people gather, work and live. The meditation was inspired from my studies with EraofPeace.org and Patricia Cota-Robles' books and CD's.

Many people are familiar with the concept of the Violet Flame. It has been around since the early 1900s. For me, learning about it and experimenting with it was life altering. At last there was a way to transmute negative energy anytime and anywhere.

The Meditation

I assume a relaxed position and close my eyes. As I close my eyes, I take a deep breath, a deep slow breath of life and then I slowly release this breath. I begin to breathe in and out in a calm and relaxed manner. As I breathe in a Blessing from Life, I exhale out a Blessing to Life. As I continue this breathing to bless myself and extend out on the exhalation a Blessing to Life, I notice a calm feeling in my body, my emotions and my mind.

I now call upon the sacred energy of the Violet Flame to blaze through me, to transmute and to forgive any mistakes I feel I have made, both those known to me and those not known to my conscious mind. I know if there is any situation keeping me from experiencing harmony within myself, I only need to ask for forgiveness in this sacred place within my heart—for I know as I forgive any person or situation that may have caused me harm, or perhaps a time where I may have caused harm to any part of life, I can now release this burden into the limitless power of forgiveness of the Violet Flame.

With my inner vision I imagine the color of violet pouring down on, around and through me, as I continue to breathe in this magnificent energy, and I exhale it out to any person, condition or situation in need of healing. It is done, and I can choose to go back and relive any perceived notions or feelings of guilt or I can switch my attention back to this moment and remind myself that I have released this burden into the sacred fire of the Violet Transmuting Flame of Forgiveness. Because I have now released my burdens, this negative energy, I now ask that my conscious mind be filled with a renewed sense of purpose and that my purpose and reasons for being here on the planet are brought into my awareness. I am now able to "see with new eyes and hear with new ears," and I know that each and every person, animal or situation in my life brings a message for me.

Part 2

Animal Communication How-To

By now you can see that Animal Communication becomes a way of life and not just something one does—it is a way of thinking and perceiving the world.

It may help if you focus on one particular type of animal when you are starting to give consults for others. A type of animal that perhaps you already know something about, so you can offer solutions to behavioral issues, because that is the reason most people call me these days. They have behavioral issues with their horse or dog. This was not so when I first started in 1996. Back then, I was called because people were curious and just wanted to see what their animal would say. Then as the years went on, and people evolved and the internet evolved, the calls I got were distress calls. Behavioral problems with horses and dogs. Nowadays, that is about 100% of the calls I get. No more curiosity seekers. Ah, relief. The media calls have died down, too, but for many years I responded and showed up for all of them.

Some Animal Communicators I know have told me of positive results for the animal just from the session itself. One lady I heard of did communication sessions with tigers and she knew virtually nothing about them, but the caretaker of the tiger saw instant results following the session in that the tiger was calmer and easier to handle.

My work is primarily with horses and big dogs because those are the animals I resonate with. If during a consult I see behavioral issues with a horse, I am able to offer solutions and often I work directly with the horse and person to help them solve their challenges.

I have a friend who knows all things cat! I do not work with cats, because I am not skilled with them, nor do I know much about their behavior. I have trouble holding my attention very long on cats; it is like there is a block there. I think deep down, I am afraid of them!

So go where your passion is and what you feel comfortable doing. Practice like I did when I was going to rodeos, and consider offering your services for free or by donation until you feel confident.

The Steps

Step 1: Begin a meditation/prayer discipline daily with a focus on fostering a relationship with the Angelic Kingdom that watches over animals. "Ask" for their assistance to come to you when you are communicating with animals.

Step 2: Become energy sensitive, if you are not already. Practice by interpreting or reading the energy of places and animals. Start to notice the changes in energy in different places, as you go about life. What are you feeling? What thoughts are coming in? What reactions are going on in your own body?

Step 3: Arrange to communicate with someone's animal—one you do not know anything about. Sit quietly with the animal and make eye contact with him/her if you can. First, give a personality reading. Describe out loud to the owner the personality qualities you perceive.

Step 4: In your thoughts or out loud, ask the animal what he/she wants the humans to know. Be open. The information usually comes quickly, in about the first four minutes of contact with an animal. This is why, when I give barn consults for several horses, I ask for the humans to please be quiet. I also have music I listen to with a headset while I am communicating with the horse. Two reasons for that: one, it blocks any human chatter and second, this music, *Medicine Woman* by Medwyn Goodall, helps me access the information I want to hear from the horse.

It comes fast for me, and sometimes I do not even know what it all means, but I usually find out when I communicate it to the owner. It is like putting a puzzle together. If the horse communicates he was injured, I tell the owner and ask if that is so.

Information, telepathically, as I said, usually comes in

the first four minutes. Listen to your thoughts, close your eyes, and see if any images are coming to you. For example, upon closing my eyes once, I was able to see in my inner vision like a replay of an accident a horse had in his past. It was like watching a movie on my own internal screen. We all have this internal screen, but if you do not see anything, that is okay, too. We are all different and access information in various ways.

Pay attention. You might get an instant flash of an image in your mind, such as the color of a dog's bed. Follow that and ask the dog, "What is it about your bed?" Talk to him/her in your thoughts or out loud and wait for a response in your own thoughts, feelings, images, and impressions.

Communicate the information you received to the animal's owner and ask the owner if the information was helpful. Consults with animals are supposed to be insightful, helpful, and also fun!

Step 5: Trust the information you receive. Train yourself to listen.

There have been times I have received information from an animal and my linear brain took over and I did not tell the owner because the information sounded useless to me. One instance was during a consult with a horse I was asked to communicate with. He showed me images of himself eating his food on the ground. If it was placed somewhere else, he would fight with his bucket to tear it down and kick it back to another place that he liked onto the dirt.

When I saw these images, and this information came to me, I took my headset off, bringing me back into this world, and thought the information was not accurate.

When the owner told me she called me for a consult specifically to find out why her horse knocks over his grain bucket, I gasped! The horse had told me that, but I did not trust the information!

So trust. The rest of this story was that I put the headset back on and walked back over to the horse. The horse looked physically fit, like he had never seen a bad day in his life. I waited and then an image of feed and dirt mixed on the ground appeared, and an image of this same horse, several hundred pounds underweight. He was a rescue horse and he was trying to tell us he felt more comfortable eating his food off the ground because what little food he got back then, was thrown on the ground.

I turned to the owner and told her what I had received. She pulled out some photos she had been given by the rescue, as she never saw him when he was starved.

Now for the solution: I advised her to halter and put a lead line on him and hold the lead line while he ate; to install the feeder bucket so it could not be easily moved.

She did this for two weeks and after that, he quit trying to knock his feed bucket down for the most part. Habits like this can run deep and can take time to fix.

Listening is perhaps the most important part of Animal Communication. The music helps me listen to my own thoughts, feelings, images, and impressions from the animal. Not everyone needs music to do this—it is just helpful for me, so I am not so distracted by the physical world.

Step 6: Discuss the information you received from the animal with the owner. Ask the owner if he/she has any questions for the animal. Facilitate a two-way conversation between the animal and the owner.

Step 7: Ethics. Once upon a time I was filmed by a TV Network performing readings on horses. There was another Animal Communicator that I had not met that this media network also interviewed and filmed. I was taken to a barn to give communication sessions for horses. That is my niche and where I am most comfortable. The filming crew did not stress or bother me.

The other lady was taken into a house with domestic animals. During her reading she started to talk about the animals' past lives. She may have been right on with her impressions, but mainstream society is usually not concerned with past lives of animals or, for that matter, past lives of people. So the information she gave had no real *value* for the owners of the animals and the news network had no problem with making that apparent.

I reached out to her, tried to call her, but was not able to get in touch with her. I wanted to help her, just as others had helped me when I started. I had been fortunate to learn early from my teachers not to reveal information of that sort because most people are looking for solutions to a problem they are having currently or they just want to enjoy the consult. Should I get an impression of a past life connection, I keep it to myself unless my client asks me. And on occasion they do ask, but I do not always know the answer. *I have to see relevance. I have to see how information can be of value and help, in the here and now.*

I did readings on several horses that day for the TV reporter. They were courteous with the camera and kept out of my immediate space. There was one particular horse that was in a stall. The barn manager asked me to do a read on him. The camera was rolling.

All I could physically see of the horse was his head and neck. I put on my music with my CD headset and approached the horse, gazing into his eyes. And as I always do, I asked the horse in my thoughts, "What is your story, what do you want us to know?" I immediately felt pain in my hips and legs, and then I saw with my inner vision an accident with what looked like fence or ropes. I took off my headset and told the barn manager what I received in this communication session. She threw her hands up and shouted, "There is no way that is true, this horse has never been injured, you are wrong!" I looked around at the news reporter and the camera crew, and of course Dano who was standing there bewildered. Dano walked over to me and said, "Honey, just let it go, you are going to ruin your career, just let her be right."

"No," I said, "I won't do it!" Looking at the barn manager, I once again denied her statement and told her I was sure that I was correct.

She argued with me, holding firm that I was wrong then she turned to the camera crew and demanded they shut it off. I heard her yell to the news reporter, "You did not tell me Catherine was going to uncover information like that!"

The barn manager was angry – I could not figure out why, but learned the reasons later. It turned out this horse was for sale and had been shipped over from another country. The news reporter called me after I left the area. She said she did her own investigation of what happened to this horse and after having contacted the horse's vet, found out the story the horse told me was true. By the way, this horse was for sale for six figures.

∽

It is easy to lose your way when you spend most of your time exploring your own multidimensional self and the realms of spirit. Balance is the key. Staying connected to the physical world we live in while staying in touch with the spiritual realms.

Probably for me, working in medicine, particularly the emergency room, helped me stay balanced although there were times, I will admit that I felt I had lost it. And, certainly, riding and having the opportunity to learn to train horses from some top horsemen, made a huge difference. I definitely would not want to be riding a horse for his/her first ride and be focused on his/her past lives! I would want to be focused on making sure that horse is comfortable and trusting me, lest I find myself thrown on the ground.

Meet your clients where they are in their thinking about life, religion, and animals. Not everyone shares the same beliefs or religious philosophy. It would be arrogant of us to try to change someone's belief system to be just like our own. Stay in the moment and stay in the energy of "how can I help this person and this animal?" Because if you cannot help, do not leave the person dismayed or confused. Be mindful of what you say and how it is perceived by the humans. People's perceptions are as variable as their fingerprints. It is all in what they hear when you speak, their perception of what you are saying.

My mind tends to work in images, pictures in my mind, so I often feel like I am stumbling with words. It takes time to see the image in my brain and then formulate words for those pictures and feelings and then to speak. I was put in speech therapy when I was a child, and I often think if they knew back then I was having trouble with getting the images and pictures into words, they would have recognized this as a processing issue, not just a speech impediment.

Also, be aware of communicating any information concerning an animal's health. Because I am a horse trainer and consultant, it is common for horse trainers to suggest medical intervention from a veterinarian or health care specialist. If I detect a medical issue, I simply ask the owner if there have been any issues and I might suggest they seek the advice of their vet. I do not diagnose or treat medical issues. Make that clear before going into a consult.

Euthanasia

I get a significant number of calls from people who are facing the choice of having their dog friends euthanized. They have usually been told by well-meaning people that "it is time." Most of these well-meaning people are ones close to the person, a husband, sister, brother or best friend. Those are powerful words when a grieving person is hearing them from people they love and trust. However, this is a time to go inward and connect with what your heart tells you. Only the dog's person should make this decision, and it grieves me when I hear these stories of my clients being told by others what to do.

If you have a friend facing this decision, the most helpful thing to do is guide him/her to the choice that feels best for that person. Saying things like, "Your dog is suffering and you must put her down" are hard to hear and only make the choice harder, unless your friend asks you. Let your friend come to the conclusion in his/her own time. Otherwise, the guilt experienced by the human will make the grieving process worse. He/she may never get over it. Encourage your friend to communicate with his/her dog friend and ask the dog if it is time.

Once the dog is gone from the physical body, everything changes for the person, immediately. I never, ever will tell someone it is time to have the dog euthanized. I will hold them, hug them, and talk to them so they can make their own decision. I also sometimes encourage them to go and talk with their veterinarian.

Sometimes clients call me to talk to their sick dog, to see if their dog is comfortable and I will do that. Mostly it is to support them and their dog during this heartbreaking time of saying goodbye.

If you know you are facing this decision, make a plan with your veterinarian. As an Animal Communicator, never predict death or tell the human what they should do. Provide support, encourage them that they are providing the comfort measures that they can. Help them brush their animal and give ice chips if needed. Give your love and understanding.

ॐ

The following is what is on my web site from about 1998 regarding my work. The fact that each animal has his or her own "story" was the basis of my consults. It was the question I always asked when I communicated with an animal. It is a very important concept to me, that each animal, just like each person, has his/her own story to tell. We can help animals by listening to their stories. How often have you felt the need to talk to someone who understands you? The animals feel the same way.

Animal Consultations

We know we are here to grow spiritually. We can help the animals, too. We have captured and domesticated wild animals. They do not speak our language. Telepathic communication sessions are a heart-to-heart talk with them, using our deepest empathy for wisdom and insight to help them. We honor them as the extensions of our family that they have come to be.

My work celebrates animals as body, mind and spirit.

In sessions, this gives me insight into their personality, and impressions of their emotional, and spiritual nature. By listening to "their story" we can further understand them and help meet their spiritual, emotional, and physical needs.

What kind of information to expect and questions I ask them:

🔵 **Insight into Personality** — my impressions of your animal's personality traits.

🔵 **Emotional Nature** — I will then ask them, "What is your story?" And I give them a chance to express their feelings, their perspective on life. Things like how they feel about the humans in their world, their home, and their friends. "What is life like for you right now? Are you happy?" And any other information they wish to communicate.

🔵 **Kindred Spirit Connections!** Helping people with their animal friends to bridge gaps in communication through better understanding by looking at life through the eyes of the animal. Your opportunity to ask your animal questions!

This is the information sheet I made and used for years. It evolved out of what I was learning from the many consults I was giving and realizing that I needed to help my clients and their animals through education. I would fill it out for each client visit.

Home Consultations with Catherine Ceci, Animal Communicator

Animal's Story:

Personality Reading of Animal:

Likes and Dislikes:

Past experiences:

Problems/Complaints from Animal's point of view:

Human's concern:

Diet/health:

Exercise:

Social life and time spent alone:

Purpose:

Sleep/rest area/crate/stall:

Play area/time:

Equipment concerns:

Possible solutions:

Practical Help:

Some of the reasons problems occur between domestic animals and humans:

1. Lack understanding of animal's personality – Gaps in understanding/communicating with each other.

2. Animal not able to adapt to human's lifestyle.

3. Human's expectations exceed animal's ability to perform.

Messages from Animals in the Wild

Dano and I had gone to the beach on Dog Island off the coast of Florida with his entire family. It was a weekend of reunion and a lot of fun. But for me, I was always stressed when I left home, concerned about not seeing my horse each day. So I had a friend stay at my house just to look after my horse.

At the beach house, I was washing the dishes while the family was visiting and catching up with each other. It was noisy. The sink was below a large window and while I was washing, suddenly, seemingly out of nowhere, a crow landed outside on the window ledge and made a loud thump into the window when he did. The family all heard it and turned their attention to me.

I looked the crow in the eyes, he was so close to me, and I was a bit shaken by his appearance and the look in his eye. I asked out loud, "What is it? Is something wrong?" And then I heard it in my thoughts, and it was very loud. The crow said, "Your horse is going to be injured, but do not worry, she will be fine. It is just a minor injury." Dano's family asked me what the crow said, some of them just making fun of me. So I told them. I repeated what the crow said. The words had hardly left my mouth when the phone rang. The friend taking care of my horse on the other end of the phone line repeated those same words. "Catherine, your horse has somehow injured her hoof. I wrapped it, and she will be fine, but I just wanted to let you know."

After that, Dano's family quit picking on me about Animal Communication. Instead, they had many questions.

There are books that explain the meaning and messages that animals bring to us. Things like an owl being an omen of something to come. Hawks have always been an important messenger bird to me, and there are traditional messages for the meaning of their visitations. I particularly like the book *Animal Speak* by Ted Andrews.

For years, I did e-mail and phone consultations helping people discover and decipher the meaning of the animals they were drawn to. My newsletter was called *Animals of Spirit* and *Animals of Spirit Readings.*

But what I learned and want to share with you that I feel is vitally important to this journey is that we can communicate directly with the animal and find out the message that is specific to us! For this has happened to me more than once. I was just as surprised with the message from the crow as Dano's family was. I truly was. Although I was giving consults for horses at this time in my life, for a crow to come to me with a message about my horse was simply amazing.

I dissected what happened.

We are where our attention is and I know my attention stays pretty much focused on nature and the animals. When the crow landed on the window and looked at me, it sure got my attention. I stayed focused on him and asked him a question and then, *I listened.*

These days, when a wild animal suddenly appears to me, I take note if they are looking right at me so I can determine if this is a personal message to me or one in the traditional sense. Reading and knowing about what some of the indigenous peoples thought about the meaning of wild animals appearing to them is definitely interesting and no doubt opened my awareness. But to have one actually communicate a personal message was a sacred honor to me.

I have shared this experience in my lectures with the emphasis on the fact that I am not special—we are all special. It is just where I place my attention. We are all capable of open-hearted telepathic communication. But is it a priority for most people? No, it is not.

Lost Animals

Some Animal communicators claim they can locate lost animals. I have had many calls regarding lost animals over the years but I do not take on these cases. I do not think I am good at that, and it would hurt to think I might have given a client any false hope.

I advise clients to participate in a meditation to their animal that is lost. It is basically a prayer to the animal to help assist him/her in coming home or finding a way to, because that is what I do should one go missing. And one did. My cat, Angel, took off for a week shortly after I found her alone in the rain under a car. She was a kitten, and I live in the woods where hawks and owls also live and hunt smaller animals.

Each night for a week, I would meditate and try to see with my inner vision where she was. I kept getting images of the woods and a path by my house. I started sending thoughts to her. I did not feel like she had passed away, but I did feel like she was lost.

A week later, she showed up at the back door, very thin and hungry. She has not left the yard since. Did the meditation work? I cannot prove that it did, but it certainly did not hurt.

I advise my clients to mediate also and see if they receive any intuitive messages to look in a certain place or go somewhere.

Many years ago, my dog PSA took off while I was out of town. My family was watching her and she managed to get away from them. I came home right away and called the animal shelter with her description. She also had on a collar. They told me she was not there. I lay on the bed sobbing and then got myself together and started meditating. I kept getting this magnetic pull to go to that same animal shelter. The linear, earth-bound part of my brain argued with me; after all, I was just told she was not there. But there was this pull directing me to go and so I did. And there was PSA!

Many years ago, I got a call from a woman who said she had heard of me and that her dog was missing. It turned out she lived just down the road from me. I told her the usual, how to meditate with her dog and to do all the practical things, such as posting signs and checking with the local shelters. She was sobbing so badly that I finally told her I would try, but that I had to be in the area the dog was last seen, which was her home. I made it clear to her that I doubted I could locate her dog and that I did not want to waste her time. I also would not accept any money for this. Feeling like maybe I could at least comfort or help her with some practical things, like taking some of her flyers to post, I went. On the way there, I was about in tears myself just knowing how upset the woman was. Along the dirt road I was travelling on, I looked to the right and a horse came running up to the fence like he was in a hurry to see me! I remember thinking, hmmmm, something is up here. I pulled my truck over, got out and walked up to him. No one else was around. He was staring at me hard; he had big, expressive, kind eyes.

I said out loud to him, "Hello there! I am on my way to help a lady who is just around the corner here. Her dog is missing. Do you know where he went?"

In my thoughts I heard, "Stand on her front porch and walk to the right through the woods. You will find him there." I thanked the horse and went around the corner and met the woman. I took her to the front porch and relayed what the horse told me. I had an appointment somewhere else and had to leave, but I gave her the instructions about which way to walk and look.

She called me later that afternoon and said they had found her dog in an abandoned shed not far from the house, precisely like the horse had said; they had followed those directions. And even better, the dog was okay.

Again, I cannot explain this all myself, but my thoughts are that a lot of it has to do with paying attention. I pay attention to the animal kingdom because that is where I feel happy and useful. Having struggled with feeling unhappy most of my life, I turned my attention to animals at a young age to find peace, but mostly to find a connection with something or someone alive, a connection that I was missing from humans.

Manifestation of a Blanket

In the 1980s, long before I began my journey as an Animal Communicator, I lived in the woods off a small highway where hunters were prevalent with their dogs. One day, as I was coming home, I saw two dogs on the side of the road. They were deer hunting dogs and it was obvious they had been hit by a car. As I pulled over, I could tell one of them was already dead. The other one lying nearby was still breathing. I knelt down by the dog that was still alive. Being cautious, as injured animals can be dangerous, I saw that his wounds were massive and was concerned if I tried to pick him up, he might bite me. There were no cell phones at that time, I was kneeling down and started sobbing. Nobody seemed interested in stopping to help me. Dead hunting dogs, run over by cars, was sadly a common site. I took my belt off my jeans and ran it through the dog's collar then realized I had nothing to drag him onto. My plan was to pull him by the collar, wrap him up and then lift him into my truck. That was when I really felt the pain and suffering of this dog, *the needless pain and suffering.* This did not have to happen but because of the greed of people who exploit dogs and leave them roaming around highways and traffic, well, it overwhelmed me. I felt so helpless. I looked up at the sky and I said out loud in a tearful voice, "God, help me. If only I had a blanket I could roll him onto— just one blanket," I shouted while sobbing. When I looked back down, there was an old brown blanket just a few feet from me and the dog. I grabbed it and pushed it under the dog and rolled him up in it and put him in my truck. It was a few miles to where I was living and all the way there I kept thinking, "Where in the world did that blanket come from?" It was not there when I pulled over, for I would have seen it!

I got home and called the other family members out. They lifted the dog out of my truck with the blanket and put him in the back of our horse trailer. One of them inquired about the blanket saying, "Cath, this is an odd looking blanket. Where did you get it?" I just muttered, "Um, well it appeared on the side of the road." The dog had a collar on, so we called a vet and we called the owner. The owner arrived and took the dog with him. I went to the horse trailer after he left, because I wanted to look at the blanket. It was not there.

Gone.

No one had touched it; the dog's owner did not take it with him. We never saw the blanket again.

Thank you for joining me on my Journey through life, through the mansions, and also for sharing your Love for the Animal Kingdom. I would love to hear your stories so please write and share with me at CatherineCeci@gmail.com or Catherine Ceci   P.O. Box 323, Lloyd, FL 32337

About the Author

Catherine Lynn Ceci is a pioneer of Equine Communication. She started giving consultations in 1996 for people and their horses and her work took her across the U.S. and to China where she taught workshops and gave consultations. From humane societies to horse clubs, churches and other groups, she shared what she has been learning about interspecies communication. With a strong background in horse training, she is able to offer solutions for horses and their owners and has been widely featured in the media both in the U.S. and China.

Catherine is also a Certified Respiratory Therapy Practitioner, working over 30 years in emergency rooms, intensive care units, nursing homes and rehabilitation centers. The pain and suffering she witnessed in her career, along with the deep sense of loss of her animals, stirred a calling in her heart to search for answers beyond traditional thinking. She is available for coaching sessions by appointment. You may contact her at

CatherineCeci@gmail.com

SpiritofHorses.com

Made in the USA
San Bernardino, CA
12 February 2017